Charlie Gets Respect

Also by the Author

Poetry

The Ant Farm

Swatting Gnats

Thirty Years in Flight (lyrics)

Children's Books

The Zoophabet

There's Poo on my Shoe

For the Young Scientist

Amoebae are not Self-Aware

Charlie Gets Respect

by

Lee Alloway

Ancient Eagle Press

Falls Church, VA

This limited edition of Charlie Gets Respect

has been printed in the United States of America for

Ancient Eagle Press.

For the Guinea Pig

Charlie Gets Respect

It was a very quiet morning in Glen Forest. Charlie the Chickadee was not singing. For years Charlie had added music to the forest, whistling at the neighboring birds and fussing at the squirrels on the bird feeder. When the blue jays came and ate all the peanuts Charlie would cuss under his breath, just loud enough to be heard by the other birds.

But now Charlie was gone. After five years in the forest…quite a long life for a chickadee…Charlie had whistled one last song before his little heart stopped and he fell from his tree.

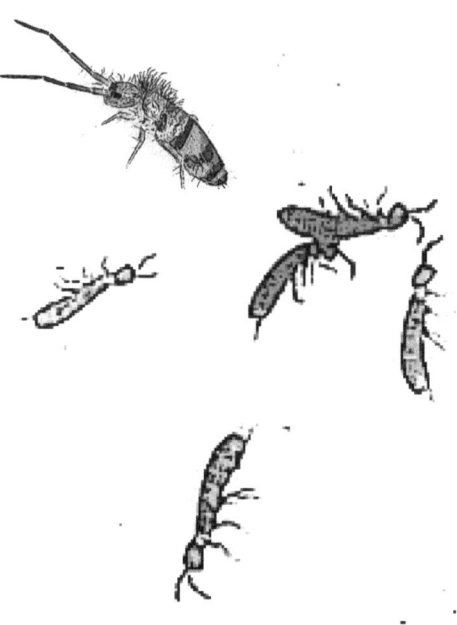

Sprocket the Springtail was the first to know.
Sprocket lived under the leaves on the ground with
his many children and extended family. He was just
sitting down to breakfast when Charlie fell on his
roof. When Sprocket discovered what had happened
he told his wife and extended family, "Charlie has
died. We must go pay our respects." And so they
did. Within a few minutes Sprocket the Springtail and
his extended family began arriving where Charlie had
fallen. They thanked Charlie for the music he had
brought to the forest over the years, then stayed to
nibble on the soil microbes that were already
digesting parts Charlie no longer needed.

An hour later Sylvester the Scuttle Fly came by. "I got wind of what happened to Charlie," he said, "and came to pay my respects." Being a scuttle fly, Sylvester showed his respect by scuttling back and forth on Charlie in his jerky way. "My, this would be a lovely place to raise a family," said Sylvester. So he called his wife Sassy who proceeded to lay eggs along Charlie's fine feathers.

The next morning Ralph and his cousin Roland the Rove Beetle arrived. "We smelled Charlie and came to pay our respects," said Roland. As rove beetles, Ralph and Roland showed their respect by munching on Charlie, a few of Sprocket the Springtail's relatives, some of Sassy the Scuttle Fly's eggs and some old leaves rotting in the corner.

As evening approached, Sassy the Scuttle Fly was frightened when a large bumble bee came zooming toward her. But it wasn't a bumble bee at all. It was Glenda, the Gold-necked Carrion Beetle. Being a gold-necked carrion beetle, Glenda was very respectful and very proper. "My, my," said Glenda. "This will never do. Charlie the Chickadee is just lying there on the ground. That is not proper at all." So Glenda got to work digging a hole under Charlie so he could settle into a proper resting place. While Glenda was digging, mites she carried on her back cleaned Charlie and left antibiotics behind so Charlie would stay fresh for Glenda's kids when they were old enough to show their own respect in a few days.

Soon Glenda the Gold-necked Carrion Beetle's cousin Carrie the American Carrion Beetle arrived, looking for a place to raise a family. Unlike her gold-necked cousin, Carrie was less polite when showing her respect. She quickly began eating everything in sight, including eggs that had been laid by earlier visitors. She, too, carried mites with her, but hers began eating eggs to reduce the competition for Carrie's future family.

The next morning Clovis the Clown Beetle came to
show his respect. Clovis was black and shiny and
very proud of his wings. He proceeded to show his
respect by recycling some of Charlie the Chickadee
and munching on some larvae that had recently
emerged. Clovis was happily browsing when he was
frightened by a pine cone falling nearby. Being a
clown beetle, he did what Clown beetles do: he
folded his legs up under him, tucked his head low and
played dead.

When a respectful time had passed, Clovis the Clown Beetle unfolded his legs and started walking when suddenly he bumped into his cousin Samantha, the Scooped Scarab Beetle. Samantha was big for a girl her age and very hairy, which is quite fashionable for scooped scarab beetles. "I recommend you try the fly larvae," Samantha said politely. "They're delicious with bits of Charlie the Chickadee on the side."

While Clovis the Clown Beetle and Samantha the Scooped Scarab Beetle quietly paid their respects, Sly the Stilt-legged Fly dropped in to check out the springtails and lick up any extra minerals that might be available. "You guys better be careful," warned Sly. "I saw the spiders coming this way. They'll be here any time now."

And sure enough, just as many of the eggs began to hatch and the larvae began to crawl, Kate the Crab Spider arrived to pay her respects, and Parker the Orb Weaver started spinning a web to capture the sweat bees that were visiting.

And so it went, with many of the bugs in Glen Forest coming to pay their respects to Charlie. As Sprocket the Springtail and his extended family munched on microbes that digested parts Charlie the Chickadee wasn't using any more, Charlie became part of them. As eggs hatched and larvae grew, they ate parts of Charlie and Charlie became part of them. As Glenda's baby Gold-necked Carrion Beetles ate the parts that the mites had cleaned, Charlie became part of them as well. And as Ralph and Roland the rove beetles munched on the other bugs, Charlie became part of them, too.

When all that was left of Charlie the Chickadee fell peacefully into the hole that Glenda the Gold-necked Carrion Beetle had properly dug for him, all the bugs that had arrived to pay their respects left, one by one. But Roland the Rove Beetle never made it home. As Roland was running between fallen leaves by the rotting stump, waiving his abdomen menacingly in the air, Charo the Chickadee swooped down and grabbed Roland (who now contained a lot of recycled Charlie) by the neck, ate his head and fed the rest of him to one of her chicks.

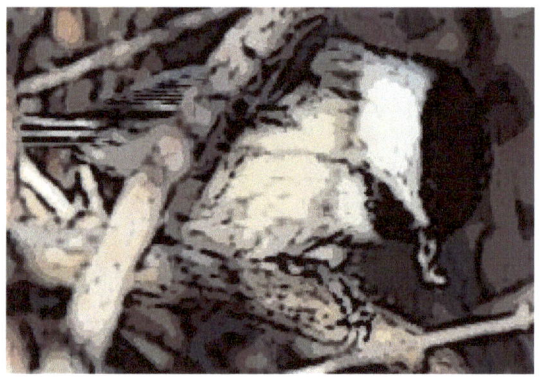

Because Charlie had gone through the soil microbes to Sprocket the Springtail to Roland the Rove Beetle to Charo and on to her chick, part of Charlie was a Chickadee again!

So when you hear a chickadee whistling at the neighboring birds, or fussing at the squirrels on the feeder, of cussing under his breath at the blue jays on the peanuts, you'll know that Charlie is back filling the forest with music, brought back to life through the respect of his friends.

The end.

Background

The events in Charlie Gets Respect occurred in a Northern Virginia backyard over six days in August 2014, but are representative of the small dramas that happen every day in every region of the world. All the bugs were photographed on site by the author and, when captured, were returned where found, confused but unharmed. The chickadee pictures, however, are not of Charlie.

The Players

Charlie – A Carolina Chickadee (*Poecile carolinensis*) of the Paridae family. At 5-inches (120 mm) and weighing only 1/3 of an ounce, the chickadee is a common sight throughout the Southeastern United States and a frequent visitor of bird feeders. Eating insects and seeds, the Chickadee is a year-round resident. It nests in tree cavities, often using former woodpecker nests, but will also use backyard nest boxes.

Sprocket – A 3mm Springtail (*Homidia sauteri*) in the *Isotomidae* family, of which 1400 species have been identified worldwide. Springtails are not insects. Although both are in the subphylum *Hexapoda*, the Springtails are in class *Entognatha* while insects are (surprise!) *Insecta*. Springtails do not directly participate in the decomposition of organic matter (e.g., Charlie); they make the process possible by controlling and harvesting soil microbes that actually do the work. Scientists estimate there are about 100,000 springtails in every cubic meter of soil in temperate climates.

Sylvester and **Sassy** – 3 mm Phorid flies (*Phoridae*) known as Scuttle Flies. Because these flies are so attracted to corpses and have a relatively well understood life cycle, they are an important tool for forensic analysis.

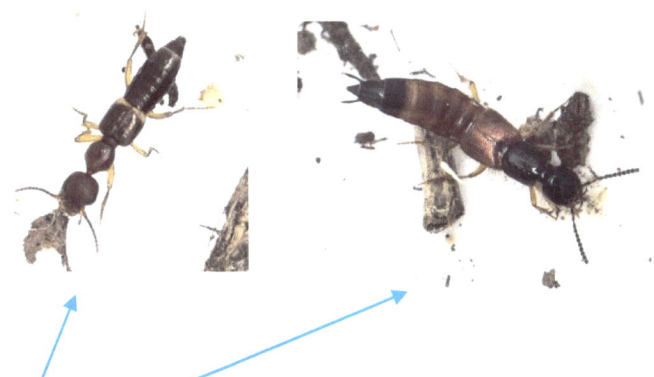

Ralph and **Roland** – 3-4 mm Rove beetles (Staphylinidae). Ralph is in the genus *Rugilus* (possibly *Rugilus angularis*) while Roland is a *Belonuchus rufipennis*. They belong to the largest family of beetles: There are more than 58,000 species of *Staphylinidae* currently identified.

A third Rove beetle (*Aleochara*) was also present. Of all the Rove beetles, only the genus *Aleochara* is parasitic. This beetle will lay her eggs on fly larva which will become nourishment for the larval beetle. Under the protective cover of their short elytra Rove beetles fold an impressive set of wings.

Glenda, the Gold-necked Carrion Beetle (*Nicrophorus tomentosus*) is a 12mm burying beetle. It excavates the area under carrion so the remains settle into a protected grave to serve as food for the next generation of carrion beetles. This interesting beetle is one of the best parents of the insect world. After eggs are laid near a carcass, both parents protect the eggs. When the eggs hatch in four days, both parents protect and feed the larva until they pupate. Factoid: *N. tomentosus* is a very smelly beetle.

Carrie – A 12 mm American Carrion Beetle (*Necrophila americana*). Unlike the more refined Gold-necked Carrion Beetle, *N. americana* feeds directly on the carcass and anything that happens to be the area. Eggs, larvae and other beetles are all on the menu for this beetle. Her eggs are laid directly on the carcass and feed on it until they drop off and pupate in the soil. This carrion beetle frequently engage in mutualistic phoresis with mites of the genus *Poecilochirus*. Most of the mites arrive and depart with the adult beetle, but some remain with the carcass and depart with the young beetles after they pupate.

Clovis – A 6 mm Clown Beetle (*Histeridae*). A common visitor to carrion, the clown beetle generally prefers to eat the eggs and larva of flies and other beetles.

Samantha – A 7 mm Scooped Scarab Beetle (*Onthophagus hecat.*) While open to eating carrion or occasional fungi, the Scooped Scarab Beetle is, after all, a dung beetle so its lunch of choice is…well…dung. Perhaps this is not the first choice of professions for everyone, but dung beetles are major contributors to the world's hygiene.

Sly – A Stilt-legged Fly (*Rainieria antennaepes*). Stilt-legged flies are wasp mimics who walk with their front legs extended, appearing like wasp antennae. *R. antennaepes* is a relatively gentle soul among the stilt-legged flies, preferring to take its nourishment from dung and detritus in the yard rather than eating other bugs. Other Stilt-legged flies would be much happier munching the springtails.

Kate – A small (5mm) Crab Spider (*Xysticus*) – Not bothering to build a web, *Xystucus* waits in high traffic areas and ambushes any suitable meal that wanders by. Large front legs and a powerful venom are the recipe for hunting success.

Parker the 6-mm Orb Weaver spins a web in areas around the carrion to trap whatever attempts to wander through.

The Sweat Bee (*Lasioglossum*, subgenus *Dialictus*) – About 200 species looking very much the same to an outsider. Occasional dinner of the orb weaver.

Also Appearing – A variety of immature sow bugs, scuttle flies, miniature spiders, fly larvae and mysterious creatures of unknown provenance.

The Author (*Homo sapien sapien*) – 1776mm – World-wide distribution. This particular specimen was born in Asia, grew up in Europe and currently resides in North America. Does not favor carrion, but may occasionally feed at fast-food establishments.

Habitat includes lakes, streams, birding hot spots, rotting logs and any place grandchildren can be found. Frequently observed with camera in hand.

Acknowledgments

Many thanks to the BugGuide community (bugguide.net) for valuable assistance in identifying and understanding the various players.

Complements to Arthur Evans for his excellent Beetles of Eastern North America (Princeton University Press, 2014, ISBN: 9780691133041), my constant companion and guide to the wonderful world of Coleoptera.

Eternal gratitude to the BugShot team of Alex Wild, Piotr Naskrecki, John Abbott and Thomas Shahan for parasitizing my brain with a fascination for the beautifully weird and weirdly beautiful world of insect macro photography.